The Secret of the Strongest Kids in the World

mBraining explained to children

Christel Land

Illustrated by Shanaka Thisara

To Fiona and Grant

may your passion and generosity
inspire generations to come

Did you ever notice that some kids, they just seem strong?
They feel really sure about things and know where they belong.
They might not have the strongest muscles, but they are strong inside.
They stand up for what they believe and take everything in their stride.

I met some kids like this one day, I asked them what they do
to be this strong and kind and sure in what they go through.
A little girl came up to me and whispered in my ear
and this is what she told me, every word that I could hear:

The different parts of your body are good at different things.
If you learn what they are, you'll know what these parts can bring.
They speak in different ways and have a loud, loud voice.
They can help you clear things up if you have a tricky choice.

Your body holds the answer to every question you might get.
So let me tell you how we listen and you will be all set.
You see, being strong means knowing all the parts of you.
You need to learn to listen well, I'll show you what to do.

Our head is good at thinking and come up with brand new things.
It gives us lots of words and it gives our ideas wings.
Our head untangles tricky thoughts and helps us understand
and that is how our head helps us think and expand.

Our heart is where we love and that's why we listen to it too.
It will tell you what you're feeling and whispers things so true.
Our heart is where we connect with others near and far
and that is how our heart helps us feel who we truly are.

Your belly helps you do the things that you want to do.
And it helps you only do the things that are really, truly you.
This is where you find the courage to be who you really are
and that is how our belly helps us be the bravest kids by far!

Now that I have told you what your different parts can do,
let me tell you how you use them to be the strongest you.
You start by being centered and calming yourself right down
and getting peace and quiet from everyone around.

Then start taking your breathing in to your deepest parts.
You'll be able to feel each breath in your belly and your heart.
Once you have found your breathing and your calm and quiet place,
you'll be ready to listen, because this takes a bit of space.

Turn your attention to your body and ask yourself deep inside
what it wants to tell you, I promise it will not hide.
Put your hand on your heart and feel what it wants to say.
If you are feeling lost your heart will always know the way.

Then focus on your head and all the ideas it can bring.
Your head can give you thoughts that are the coolest thing.
Then put your hands on your belly and listen to this part of you.
It might surprise you how much wisdom your belly can get through.

There is one thing you need to know about how the heart and belly speak,
because if you listen for words you won't hear a squeak.
These parts of you might speak in a feeling or picture or colour.
Just because they don't use words doesn't make their message any smaller.

As you go around your body, you will feel it tell you things
and this is the best place for your choices to spring.
You see, this is how we feel strong in the choices that we face,
so as you go around your body, ask these questions in your own pace:

Does my heart feel happy, does it love this new idea?
Does my head understand it, when it's whispered in my ear?
Does my belly feel safe, does it feel strong and free?
Does it feel like this choice is truly, deeply me?

If your heart, head and belly all agree on what is true,
then you will feel strong and safe and know exactly what to do.
But if they don't agree or if you ever feel in doubt,
you might feel like this is what they're trying to shout out:

My heart doesn't love it, my head can't understand!
My belly feels scared, and this isn't what I planned!
There's just something about this that doesn't feel right!
And if I choose to do this, I won't feel strong and bright!

If this is how you feel, then don't go anywhere.
Stay where you are and give yourself lots and lots of care.
Just keep listening until you find a choice that's right for you.
It might take a little longer, but you'll feel like you just grew.

Just keep asking your body what it feels, wants and needs
and listen what it tells you until your different parts agree.
Once you have made your choice in a strong and centered way,
you'll feel kind and brave and ready, and more than just okay.

The girl pointed to her friend, he came over to say hi.
He wanted to tell me something too, but felt a little shy.

He said:

This helps me feel kind to myself and everyone around.
It makes me feel curious about the ideas I have found.
This makes me feel brave to do the things I want to do,
and helps me do those things in the best of ways too.

I really wish that more kids would be strong in this way.
I don't want this to be a secret, I wish everyone felt brave!
So now that we have told you, do you think that you could write
this secret down for every kid, so they can also feel strong and bright?

I promised them to write this down for every kid in every land.

So it can help children all around the world to truly understand

how to be strong and kind and centered in everything they do.

The next time you have a choice to make, will you try it too?

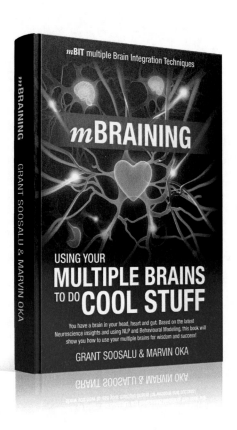

If you are a grownup and want to learn more about mBraining, you can find the original book by Grant Soosalu and Marvin Oka on Amazon.

Or go to www.mbraining.com

Other books by Christel Land

The Superhero Brain
Explaining Autism to Empower Kids

The Superhero Heart
Explaining Autism to Family and Friends

Superhero Guts
An Everyday Poem for Special Needs Parents

Made in the USA
San Bernardino, CA
25 March 2019

This rhyming story gives children a simple method for making authentic and values-based decisions. The story uses the neuroscience-based coaching technique mBraining, or mBIT, to offer children a simple but powerful way to make decisions that are right for them. The child is encouraged to listen to different parts of the body; to tune in to the heart for emotion, the head for logic and the gut for instinct.

This book is written by a mother of two, who is also a certified mBIT Trainer and Master Coach.

ISBN 9781729027882

90000

9 781729 027882